Top 50
SQL
Tricky
Interview
Questions
& Answers

Knowledge Powerhouse

DEDICATION

To our readers!

CONTENTS

1.   Write SQL query to get the second highest salary among all Employees?   **11**

2.   How can we retrieve alternate records from a table in Oracle?   **13**

3.   Write a SQL Query to find Max salary and Department name from each department.   **14**

4.   Write a SQL query to find records in Table A that are not in Table B without using **NOT IN** operator.
     15

5.   What is the result of following query?   **17**

6.   Write SQL Query to find employees that have same name and email.   **18**

7.   Write a SQL Query to find Max salary from each department.   **19**

8.   Write SQL query to get the nth highest salary among all Employees.   **20**

9.   How can you find 10 employees with **Odd** number as Employee ID?   **22**

10. Write a SQL Query to get the names of employees whose date of birth is between 01/01/1990 to 31/12/2000.   **23**

11. Write a SQL Query to get the Quarter from date.
     24

12. Write Query to find employees with duplicate

email. 25

14. Is it safe to use ROWID to locate a record in Oracle SQL queries? 26

15. What is a Pseudocolumn? 27

16. What are the reasons for de-normalizing the data? 28

17. What is the feature in SQL for writing If/Else statements? 28

18. What is the difference between DELETE and TRUNCATE in SQL? 29

19. What is the difference between DDL and DML commands in SQL? 30

20. Why do we use Escape characters in SQL queries? 32

21. What is the difference between Primary key and Unique key in SQL? 32

22. What is the difference between INNER join and OUTER join in SQL? 33

23. What is the difference between Left OUTER Join and Right OUTER Join? 36

24. What is the datatype of ROWID? 39

25. What is the difference between where clause and having clause? 39

26. What is cardinality in SQL? 40

27. What is Merge statement in SQL? 41

28. What is the difference between UNION and
UNION ALL?   42

29. What will be the result of following query?   43

30. What is the wrong with this SQL query?   45

31. What is wrong with this query to get the list of
employees not in Dept 1?   46

32. What is the use of Execution plan in SQL?   48

33. How many records are returned by following
query?   48

34. Write a query for this problem?   49

35. Write SQL Query to get Employee Name,
Manager ID and number of employees in the
department?   51

36. Write SQL Query to find duplicate rows in a
database?   52

37. Write SQL query to delete duplicate rows in a
table?   53

38. Why is the difference between NVL and NVL2
functions in SQL?   55

39. What are ACID properties in a SQL transaction?
    56

40. What is the main difference between RANK and
DENSE_RANK functions in Oracle?   57

41. What is the use of WITH clause in SQL?   58

42. Which SQL feature can be used to view data in a

table sequentially?   **60**

43. Write SQL Query to get Student Name and
number of Students in same grade.   **60**

44. Write SQL Query to get the list of grades with
total score more than average score.   **61**

45. What are the differences between CASE and
DECODE in SQL?   **63**

46. Write a Query to get Unique names of products
without using DISTINCT keyword.   **64**

47. Write a SQL query to maximum Zipcode from a
table without using MAX or MIN aggregate
functions.   **65**

48. Given a list of student names and grade. Write a
query to print a comma separated list of student
names in a grade.   **66**

49. What is the difference between Correlated and
Un-correlated Sub query?   **68**

50. Given an Employee table with Manager_ID as
column, print First name, Manager ID and Level of
employees in Organization Structure?   **69**

Bonus Question: **71**

51. Write a query to create an empty table from an
existing table?   **71**

ACKNOWLEDGMENTS

We thank our readers who constantly send feedback and reviews to motivate us in creating these useful books with the latest information!

INTRODUCTION

This book contains tricky and nasty SQL interview questions that an interviewer asks. It is a compilation of advanced SQL interview questions after attending dozens of technical interviews in top-notch companies like- Oracle, Google, Ebay, Amazon etc.

Each question is accompanied with an answer because you want to save your time while preparing for an interview.

The difficulty rating on these Questions varies from a Junior level programmer to Architect level.

Once you go through them in the first pass, mark the questions that you could not answer by yourself. Then, in second pass go through only the difficult questions.

After going through this book 2-3 times, you will be very well prepared to face a technical interview on SQL for an experienced programmer.

SQL Tricky Interview Questions

1. Write SQL query to get the second highest salary among all Employees?

Given a Employee Table with two columns

ID, Salary

10, 2000

11, 5000

12, 3000

Answer:

There are multiple ways to get the second highest salary

among all Employees.

Option 1: Use Subquery

SELECT MAX(Salary)

FROM Employee

WHERE Salary NOT IN (SELECT MAX(Salary) FROM Employee);

In this approach, we are getting the maximum salary in a subquery and then excluding this from the rest of the resultset.

Option 2: Use Not equals

select MAX(Salary) from Employee

WHERE Salary <> (select MAX(Salary) from Employee)

This is same as option 1 but we are using <> instead of NOT IN.

2. How can we retrieve alternate records from a table in Oracle?

We can use rownum and MOD function to retrieve the alternate records from a table.

To get Even number records:

SELECT *

FROM (SELECT rownum, ID, Name

       FROM Employee)

WHERE MOD(rownum,2)=0

To get Odd number records:

SELECT *

FROM (SELECT rownum, ID, Name

FROM Employee)

WHERE MOD(rownum,2)=1

3. Write a SQL Query to find Max salary and Department name from each department.

Given a Employee table with three columns

ID, Salary, DeptID

10, 1000, 2

20, 5000, 3

30, 3000, 2

Department table with two columns:

ID, DeptName

1, Marketing

2, IT

3, Finance

Answer:

This is a trick question. There can be some department without any employee. So we have to ask interviewer if they expect the name of such Department also in result.

If yes then we have to join Department table with Employee table by using foreign key DeptID. We have to use LEFT OUTER JOIN to print all the departments.

Query would be like as follows:

SELECT d.DeptName, MAX(e.Salary)

FROM Department d LEFT OUTER JOIN Employee e

ON e.DeptId = d.ID

GROUP BY DeptName

4. Write a SQL query to find records in Table A that are not in Table B without using NOT IN operator.

Consider two tables

Table_A

10

20

30

Table_B

15

30

45

Answer: We can use MINUS operator in this case for Oracle and EXCEPT for SQL Server.

Query will be as follows:

SELECT * FROM Table_A

MINUS

SELECT * FROM Table_B

5. What is the result of following query?

SELECT

    CASE WHEN null = null

    THEN 'True'

    ELSE 'False'

END AS Result;

Answer: In SQL null can not be compared with itself. There fore null = null is not true. We can compare null with a non-null value to check whether a value is not null.

Therefore the result of above query is False.

The correct way to check for null is to use IS NULL clause.

Following query will give result True.

SELECT

CASE WHEN null IS NULL

THEN 'True'

ELSE 'False'

END AS Result;

6. Write SQL Query to find employees that have same name and email.

Employee table:

ID	NAME	EMAIL
10	John	jbaldwin
20	George	gadams
30	John	jsmith

Answer: This is a simple question with one trick. The trick here is to use **Group by on two columns** Name and Email.

Query would be as follows:

SELECT name, email, COUNT(*)

FROM Employee

GROUP BY name, email

HAVING

COUNT(*) > 1

7. Write a SQL Query to find Max salary from each department.

Given a Employee table with three columns

ID, Salary, DeptID

10, 1000, 2

20, 5000, 3

30, 3000, 2

Answer:

We can first use group by DeptID on Employee table and then get the Max salary from each Dept group.

SELECT   DeptID, MAX(salary)

FROM   Employee

GROUP BY   DeptID

8. Write SQL query to get the nth highest salary among all Employees.

Given a Employee Table with two columns

ID, Salary

10, 2000

11, 5000

12, 3000

Answer:

Option 1: Use Subquery

We can use following sub query approach for this:

SELECT *

FROM Employee emp1

WHERE (N-1) = (

SELECT COUNT(DISTINCT(emp2.salary))

FROM Employee emp2

WHERE emp2.salary > emp1.salary)

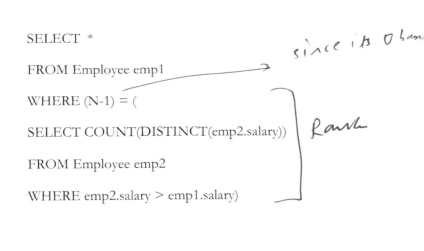

since it 0 base

Rank

Option 2: Using Rownum in Oracle

SELECT * FROM (

  SELECT emp.*,

row_number() OVER (ORDER BY salary DESC) rnum

FROM Employee emp

)

WHERE rnum = n;

9. How can you find 10 employees with Odd number as Employee ID?

Answer:

In Oracle we can use Top to limit the number of records. We can also use Rownum < 11 to get the only 10 or less number of records.

To find the Odd number Employee ID, we can use % function.

Sample Query with TOP:

SELECT TOP 10 ID FROM Employee WHERE ID % 2 = 1;

Sample Query with ROWNUM:

SELECT ID FROM Employee WHERE ID % 2 = 1
AND ROWNUM < 11;

10. Write a SQL Query to get the names of employees whose date of birth is between 01/01/1990 to 31/12/2000.

This SQL query appears a bit tricky. We can use
BETWEEN clause to get all the employees whose date of
birth lies between two given dates.

Query will be as follows:

SELECT EmpName

FROM Employees

WHERE birth_date BETWEEN '01/01/1990' AND
'31/12/2000'

Remember BETWEEN is always inclusive of both the dates.

11. Write a SQL Query to get the Quarter from date.

Answer: We can use to_char function with 'Q' option for quarter to get quarter from a date.

Use TO_CHAR with option 'Q' for Quarter

SELECT TO_CHAR(TO_DATE('3/31/2016', 'MM/DD/YYYY'), 'Q')

AS quarter

FROM DUAL

12. Write Query to find employees with duplicate email.

Employee table:

ID	NAME	EMAIL
10	John	jsmith
20	George	gadams
30	Jane	jsmith

Answer: We can use Group by clause on the column in which we want to find duplicate values.

Query would be as follows:

SELECT name, COUNT(email)

FROM Employee

GROUP BY email

HAVING (COUNT(email) > 1)

13. Write a Query to find all Employee whose name contains the word "Rich", regardless of case. E.g. Rich, RICH, rich.

Answer:

We can use UPPER function for comparing the both sides with uppercase.

SELECT *

FROM Employees

WHERE UPPER(emp_name) like '%RICH%'

14. Is it safe to use ROWID to locate a record in Oracle SQL queries?

ROWID is the physical location of a row. We can do very fast lookup based on ROWID. In a transaction where we first search a few rows and then update them one by one, we can use ROWID.

But ROWID of a record can change over time. If we rebuild a table a record can get a new ROWID.

If a record is deleted, its ROWID can be given to another record.

So it is not recommended to store and use ROWID in long term. It should be used in same transactions.

15.   What is a Pseudocolumn?

A Pseudocolumn is like a table column, but it is not stored in the same table. We can select from a Pseudocolumn, but we can not insert, update or delete on a Pseudocolumn.

A Pseudocolumn is like a function with no arguments.

Two most popular Pseudocolumns in Oracle are ROWID and ROWNUM.

NEXTVAL and CURRVAL are also pseudo columns.

16. What are the reasons for de-normalizing the data?

We de-normalize data when we need better performance. Sometimes there are many joins in a query due to highly normalized data.

In that case, for faster data retrieval it becomes essential to de-normalize data.

17. What is the feature in SQL for writing If/Else statements?

In SQL, we can use CASE statements to write If/Else statements.

We can also use DECODE function in Oracle SQL for writing simple If/Else logic.

18. What is the difference between DELETE and TRUNCATE in SQL?

Main differences between DELETE and TRUNCATE commands are:

I. **DML vs. DDL**: DELETE is a Data Manipulation Language (DML) command. TRUNCATE is a Data Definition Language (DDL) command.

II. **Number of Rows**: We can use DELETE command to remove one or more rows from a table. TRUNCATE command will remove all the rows from a table.

III. **WHERE clause**: DELETE command provides support for WHERE clause that can be used to filter the data that we want to delete. TRUNCATE command can only delete all the rows. There is no WHERE clause in TRUNCATE command.

IV. **Commit**: After DELETE command we have to issue COMMIT or ROLLBACK command to confirm our changes. After TRUNCATE command there is no need to run COMMIT. Changes done by TRUNCATE command can not be rolled back.

19. What is the difference between DDL and DML commands in SQL?

Main differences between Data Definition Language (DDL) and Data Manipulation Language (DML) commands are:

I.   **DDL vs. DML**: DDL statements are used for creating and defining the Database structure. DML statements are used for managing data within Database.

II. **Sample Statements**: DDL statements are CREATE, ALTER, DROP, TRUNCATE, RENAME etc. DML statements are SELECT, INSERT, DELETE, UPDATE, MERGE, CALL etc.

III. **Number of Rows**: DDL statements work on whole table. CREATE will a create a new table. DROP will remove the whole table. TRUNCATE will delete all records in a table. DML statements can work on one or more rows. INSERT can insert one or more rows. DELETE can remove one or more rows.

IV.   **WHERE clause**: DDL statements do not have a WHERE clause to filter the data. Most of DML statements support filtering the data by WHERE clause.

V.   **Commit**: Changes done by a DDL statement can not be rolled back. So there is no need to issue a COMMIT or ROLLBACK command after DDL statement. We need to run COMMIT or ROLLBACK to confirm our changed after running a DML statement.

VI.   **Transaction**: Since each DDL statement is permanent, we can not run multiple DDL statements in a group like Transaction. DML statements can be run in a Transaction. Then we can COMMIT or ROLLBACK this group as a transaction. E.g. We can insert data in two tables and commit it together in a transaction.

VII.   **Triggers**: After DDL statements no triggers are fired. But after DML statements relevant triggers can be fired.

20. Why do we use Escape characters in SQL queries?

In SQL, there are certain special characters and words that are reserved for special purpose. E.g. & is a reserved character.

When we want to use these special characters in the context of our data, we have to use Escape characters to pass the message to database to interpret these as non Special / non Reserved characters.

21. What is the difference between Primary key and Unique key in SQL?

Main differences between Primary key and Unique key in SQL are:

I. **Number**: There can be only one Primary key in a table. There can be more than one Unique key in a table.

II. **Null value**: In some DBMS Primary key cannot be NULL. E.g. MySQL adds NOT NULL to Primary key. A Unique key can have null values.

III.   **Unique Identifier**: Primary Key is a unique identifier of a record in database table. Unique key can be null and we may not be able to identify a record in a unique way by a unique key

IV.   **Changes**: It is not recommended to change a Primary key. A Unique key can be changed much easily.

V.   **Usage**: Primary Key is used to identify a row in a table. A Unique key is used to prevent duplicate non-null values in a column.

22.   What is the difference between INNER join and OUTER join in SQL?

Let say we have two tables X and Y.

The result of an INNER JOIN of X and Y is X intersect. It is the INNER overlapping intersection part of a Venn diagram.

The result of an OUTER JOIN of X and Y is X union Y. It is the OUTER parts of a Venn diagram.

E.g.

Consider following two tables, with just one column x and y:

```
x   |  y
- - -|- -
10  |  30
20  |  40
30  |  50
40  |  60
```

In above tables (10,20) are unique to table X, (30,40) are common, and (50,60) are unique to table Y.

INNER JOIN

An INNER JOIN by using following query will give the intersection of the two tables X and Y. The intersection is the common data between these tables.

select * from X INNER JOIN Y on X.x = Y.y;

```
x  | y
--- +--
30 | 30
40 | 40
```

OUTER JOIN

A full OUTER JOIN by using following query will us the union of X and Y. It will have all the rows in X and all the rows in Y. If some row in X has not corresponding value in Y, then Y side will be null, and vice versa.

select * from X FULL OUTER JOIN Y on X.x = Y.y;

```
x    | y
----- + -----
10 | null
```

```
20 |  null

30 |   30

40 |   40

null |   60

null |   50
```

23.   What is the difference between Left OUTER Join and Right OUTER Join?

Let say we have two tables X and Y.

The result of an LEFT OUTER JOIN of X and Y is all rows of X and common rows between X and Y.

The result of an RIGHT OUTER JOIN of X and Y is all rows of Y and common rows between X and Y.

E.g.

Consider following two tables, with just one column x and y:

```
x   |  y
- - -|- -
10  |  30
20  |  40
30  |  50
40  |  60
```

In above tables (10,20) are unique to table X, (30,40) are common, and (50,60) are unique to table Y.

LEFT OUTER JOIN

A left OUTER JOIN by using following query will give us all rows in X and common rows in X and Y.

select * from X LEFT OUTER JOIN Y on X.x = Y.y;

```
x   | y
-- -+-----
10  | null
20  | null
30  |   30
40  |   40
```

RIGHT OUTER JOIN

A right OUTER JOIN by using following query will give all rows in Y and common rows in X and Y.

select * from X RIGHT OUTER JOIN Y on X.x = Y.y;

```
x    | y
----- +----
30   |  30
40   |  40
```

null | 50

null | 60

24. What is the datatype of ROWID?

ROWID Pseudocolumn in Oracle is of ROWID datatype. It is a string that represents the address of a row in the database.

25. What is the difference between where clause and having clause?

We use where clause to filter elements based on some criteria on individual records of a table.

E.g. We can select only employees with first name as John.

SELECT ID, Name

FROM Employee

WHERE name = 'John'

We use having clause to filter the groups based on the values of aggregate functions.

E.g. We can group by department and only select departments that have more than 10 employees.

SELECT deptId, count(1)

FROM Employee

GROUP BY deptId HAVING count(*) > 10.

26.   What is cardinality in SQL?

In SQL, Cardinality is the uniqueness of data values in a column. If cardinality is low then a column will have more duplicated values.

Database use Cardinality of a column to determine the optimal query plan for a query.

of elements in a set. Thinking in the database world, cardinality has to do with the counts in a relationship, one-to-one, one-to-many, or many-to-many.

27. What is Merge statement in SQL?

Merge statement is a combination of INSERT and UPDATE statements. If data is already present in a table, it can update the existing data. If data is not present in a table, then it can insert the data.

Merge is a DML statement. So we need to run commit or rollback command after this.

Sample syntax for MERGE is:

MERGE

    INTO target_table tg_table

    USING source_table src_table

    ON (src_table.id = tg_table.id)

WHEN MATCHED

THEN

  UPDATE

  SET   tg_table.name = src_table.name

WHEN NOT MATCHED

THEN

  INSERT (tg_table.id, tg_table.name)

  VALUES (src_table.id, src_table.name);

28.   What is the difference between UNION and UNION ALL?

Main difference between UNION and UNION ALL is that UNION removes duplicate records, but UNION ALL does not remove duplicate records.

E.g. Consider two tables A and B

A   B

10   15

20   20

UNION of A and B = 10, 20, 15

UNION ALL of A and B = 10, 20, 15, 20

Performance of UNION ALL is considered better than UNION, since UNION ALL does not require additional work of removing duplicates.

29. What will be the result of following query?

Consider following tables:

Employee

ID | Emp_name

1 | Jane

2 | George

3 | John

Department

ID | Dept_name | Emp_id

1 | Marketing | 1

2 | Finance | 2

3 | Technology | null

SELECT *

FROM Employee

WHERE id NOT IN (SELECT Emp_id

    FROM Department)

Answer: The above query will return no records. The reason for this is presence of null value in Emp_id column of Department table.

When we do SELECT Emp_id FROM Department, we get null value also. Now in main query we compare NOT IN with null value, then it does not return any result.

The correct query is:

SELECT *

FROM Employee

WHERE id NOT IN (SELECT Emp_id

    FROM Department WHERE Emp_id IS NOT
NULL)

30. What is the wrong with this SQL query?

SELECT Id, to_date(OrderDate,'YYYY') AS OrderYear

FROM Order

WHERE OrderYear >= 2015;

Answer:

In the above query, OrderYear is an alias for
to_date(OrderDate,'YYYY') in SELECT clause.

When we are using OrderYear in WHERE clause, it is not available there.

Following is correct query:

SELECT Id, YEAR(OrderDate) AS OrderYear

FROM Order

WHERE YEAR(OrderDate) >= 2015;

31. What is wrong with this query to get the list of employees not in Dept 1?

SELECT Name

FROM Employee

WHERE DeptID <> 1;

Employee Table:

Id   Name   DeptID

1	John	NULL
2	George	2
3	Smith	1
4	Ray	NULL

Answer:

There are 3 Employees (John, George and Ray) not in Dept 1. But Query returns only one result: George.

Since we are just looking for employees not in Dept 1, query does not compare DeptID with NULL. So Employees without a department are not returned.

Correct Query is as follows:

SELECT Name

FROM Employee

WHERE DeptID IS NULL

OR DeptID <> 1;

1. FROM
2. WHERE
3. GROUP BY
4. HAVING
5. [SELECT] → 6. window function
7. ORDER BY

32. What is the use of Execution plan in SQL?

In an RDBMS, Execution plan is the set of steps that are executed in a specific order to get the results of a query.

Execution plan is used mainly for performance improvement of queries. It helps developers and DBAs to see the internal steps that take place during a query execution.

Based on the steps in Execution plan, we can alter the plan to include or exclude some steps or use some index etc. This helps in Query tuning and Query optimization for SQL queries.

33. How many records are returned by following query?

Table: Customer (Id, Name) has 3 records

Table: Order (Id, Order_Date) has 15 records

Select * From Customer, Order

Answer:

45

Above query returns 15 records. This is also known as Cartesian Product.

For a table with N records and another table with M records. Cartesian Product has N * M number of records.

34. Write a query for this problem?

Given a table Employee in which we have DeptId for each employee. Write a single SQL query to move the employees from DeptID 1 to 2 and move employees from DeptId 2 to 1.

Employee

Id Name DeptId

1 John   1

2	George	2
3	Jane	1
4	Smith	2

Answer:

We can use CASE statement here.

UPDATE Employee SET DeptId =

    CASE DeptId

        WHEN '1' THEN '2'

        WHEN '2' THEN '1'

      ELSE DeptId END;

35. Write SQL Query to get Employee Name, Manager ID and number of employees in the department?

Given Employee Table:

ID	NAME	MGR_ID	DEPTID
1	John	3	10
2	Smith	3	10
3	Jane	4	20

Answer: We can use WITH clause and SELF JOIN to get the required data. By WITH clause we get the count of employees in each department. Then we use SELF JOIN to get name of Manager because manager is also an employee.

Query will be as follows:

WITH d_count AS (

SELECT deptID, COUNT(*) AS d_count

FROM   employee

GROUP BY deptno)

SELECT e.name AS Employee_name,

m.name AS Manager_name

dc.d_count AS Dept_count

FROM   employee e,

d_count dc,

employee m

WHERE e.deptID = dc.deptID

AND   e.mgrID = m.ID;

36. Write SQL Query to find duplicate rows in a database?

Answer: To find duplicate rows, we have to ask the interviewer what is the criteria for considering two rows duplicate of each other.

Let say in a given table Test_table if column_1 and column_2 of two rows are same, then these rows are considered equal.

We can use GROUP BY clause to group the rows with columns that are used for checking equality. Any group that have more than 1 rows will have duplicate rows.

Query to find duplicate will be as follows:

SELECT column_1, coulmn_2, count(*)

FROM Test_table

GROUP BY column_1, coulmn_2

HAVING count(*) > 1

37.   Write SQL query to delete duplicate rows in a table?

Answer: To delete duplicate rows we need to first define the criteria for considering two rows duplicate of each other.

Let say in a given table Test_table if column_1 and column_2 of two rows are same, then these rows are considered equal.

In Oracle we can use rowid of two rows to find that these rows are different.

Query to delete duplicate rows will be as follows:

DELETE FROM

   Test_table a

WHERE

  a.rowid >

   ANY (

    SELECT

     b.rowid

   FROM

    Test_table b

   WHERE

    a.column_1 = b.column_1

AND

a.column_2 = b.column_2

);

38.   Why is the difference between NVL and NVL2 functions in SQL?

We use NVL and NVL2 functions to check if a value is NULL or not. Both these functions can be replaced with DECODE or CASE statements.

In NVL(item_to_check, alternate_value) function there are two arguments. If item_to_check is null then alternate_value is returned. If item_to_check is not null, then item_to_check is returned.

In NVL2(item_to_check, alternate_value1, alternate_value2) function there are three arguments. If item_to_check is null then alternate_value2 is returned. If item_to_check is not null, then alternate_value1 is returned. It is a short IF then ELSE statement.

39. What are ACID properties in a SQL transaction?

ACID properties stand for Atomicity, Consistency, Isolation and Durability.

A Transaction is considered reliable, if it has these characteristics.

I. **Atomicity**: It means all or nothing. A transaction is Atomic, if any part of transaction fails, then whole of the transaction is rolled back. If all the parts of transaction are successful, then only Transaction is committed.

II. **Consistency**: It means that each Transaction will ensure that Database remains in a valid state. Once the Transaction is complete, it should satisfy all the constraints, triggers, rules etc.

III. **Isolation**: It means that each transaction can be executed in separately. So it is possible to run a

transaction in a concurrent system. An incomplete
transaction is not visible to another transaction.

IV.   **Durability**: It means that changes done by a
       Transaction are permanent. Even if the Database
       crashes or power goes off, the committed
       Transaction and its results remain stored
       permanently.

40.   What is the main difference between RANK and DENSE_RANK functions in Oracle?

Both RANK and DENSE_RANK functions are used to
get the ranking of an ordered partition.

Main difference between RANK and DENSE_RANK
functions is in the handling of case when a tie happens
while ranking the data.

In a tie, RANK function skips the next ranking(s) and
assigns same rank to values that tie. So there will be gaps in
the rank.

In a tie, DENSE_RANK function does not skip the ranks. It assigns same rank to values that tie. But next rank will be consecutive rank.

E.g. In set (10, 10, 20, 30, 30, 40), RANK returns (1,1,3,4,4,6)

DENSE_RANK returns (1,1,2,3,3,4)

41. What is the use of WITH clause in SQL?

In SQL, WITH clause is used to create a Subquery or View for a set of data.

The main uses of WITH clause are:

I. **Simplify**: It can simplify a SQL query by creating a subset of data.
II. **Reduce Repetition**: WITH clause can create a subset of data that can be reused multiple times in the main query.

E.g. In following query we use WITH clause to get the set of employee in Finance department. Then we use this subset fin_employee to filter based on AGE less than 30 and Female Gender.

We have used the same set fin_employee multiple times in main query.

WITH fin_employee AS

      (SELECT *

      FROM Employee

      WHERE dep_name = 'Finance')

SELECT *

FROM fin_employee

WHERE AGE < 30

      UNION ALL

SELECT *

FROM fin_employee

WHERE Gender = 'Female';

42. Which SQL feature can be used to view data in a table sequentially?

In this question, we need to clarify with interviewer if it is about SEQUENCE based on some value in data or it is just a SEQUENCE of rows from data.

In first case, we can use ORDER BY clause in SQL to view data in a sequential order based on a value.

In second case, we can use a CURSOR to view the whole data set in a sequence.

43. Write SQL Query to get Student Name and number of Students in same grade.

Given Student Table

ID	Name	Grade
1	George	1
2	Smith	2

Answer: We can use WITH clause for this problem. We first get the number students in each grade by using GROUP BY on grade. Then we use Sub-Query returned by WITH clause in Main query.

Query will be as follows:

```
WITH grade_count AS (

  SELECT grade, COUNT(*) AS grade_count

  FROM   student

  GROUP BY grade)

SELECT s.name AS student_name,

    gc.grade_count AS grade_count

FROM   student s,

    grade_count gc

WHERE  e.grade = gc.grade;
```

44. **Write SQL Query to get the list of grades with total score more than average score.**

Consider Student and Grade tables

Student: ID, name, grade_ID, score

Grade: ID, grade_num

Answer: We can use WITH clause to get the total score in each grade. We can also use WITH clause to get the average score among all grades. Then we can use the two sub-queries to get the list of GRADES with Score total more than average score.

Query will be as follows:

```
WITH
  grade_score AS (
    SELECT grade_num, SUM(s.score) grade_total
    FROM   student s, grade g
    WHERE  s.grade_ID = g.ID
    GROUP BY grade_num),
  avg_score AS (
    SELECT SUM(grade_total)/COUNT(*) avg
    FROM   grade_score)
```

SELECT *

FROM   grade_score

WHERE   grade_total > (SELECT avg FROM avg_score)

ORDER BY grade_num;

45. What are the differences between CASE and DECODE in SQL?

Main differences between Case and Decode statements are:

I.   **Easier to Read:** CASE is more flexible and easier to read than DECODE.

II. **ANSI Compatible**: CASE is an ANSI standard. But DECODE is internal to Oracle.

III. **Location**: DECODE is used only inside SQL statement. We can use CASE any where in SQL, even as a parameter of a function/procedure.

IV. **Check**: DECODE works on the basis of an equality check. CASE can do many types of logical comparisons like < > etc.

V. **Decision Making**: We can not use complex decision making statements in a DECODE function. We cannot do decode(price = 100,'cheap',10000,'expensive','ok')

VI. **Different Types**; DECODE can take different types of expressions. But CASE has only one type of expression.

46. Write a Query to get Unique names of products without using DISTINCT keyword.

We can use GROUP BY for this purpose. It can print the distinct groups of PRODUCT NAME.

SELECT prod_name

FROM product

GROUP BY prod_name

(47.) Write a SQL query to maximum Zipcode from a table without using MAX or MIN aggregate functions.

Consider Zipcode_list table with column Zipcode

ZIPCODE

7500

7525

7550

7600

7575

Answer: Point to be noted is that the Maximum zipcode is not smaller than any Zipcode in the list.

We can use self join to find the list of Zipcodes that are smaller than at least one other Zipcode. Once we get that list, we just use NOT IN to find the Zipcode from Zipcode_list that does not exist in this smaller list. That will be the maximum Zipcode with no Zipcode bigger than it.

Query will be as follows:

SELECT DISTINCT Zipcode

FROM Zipcode_list

WHERE Zipcode NOT IN (

    SELECT Smaller_list.Zipcode

    FROM Zipcode_list AS Larger_list

    JOIN Zipcode_list AS Smaller_list

        ON Smaller_list.Zipcode <
Largerlist.Zipcode

)

48. Given a list of student names and grade. Write a query to print a comma separated list of student names in a grade.

Students

Grade	Name
1	John
1	George
1	Jane
2	Smith

2 | Anne

2 | Scott

3 | Larry

3 | Bill

Answer:

We can use LISTAGG function in Oracle for this purpose. It can transpose rows to column type values. We can set the delimiter as comma in LISTAGG function. And then we can group the students by using Grade in GROUP BY clause.

Query will be as follows:

SELECT grade, LISTAGG(name, ',') WITHIN GROUP (ORDER BY name) AS Students

FROM   student

GROUP BY grade;

Grade Students

---------- ---

1 John,George,Jane

2 Smith,Anne,Scott

3 Larry,Bill

49.   What is the difference between Correlated and Un-correlated Sub query?

When we write a subquery in such a way that inner subquery and outer main query are interdependent, then we call it s correlated Sub query. In this case, for executing every row of inner query, the outer query is also executed. The inner query needs data from the outer query for its execution.

E.g.

SELECT e.emp_name

FROM employee e

WHERE e.id = (SELECT d.emp_id

        FROM dept d

        WHERE d.dept_id = e.dept_id);

In a non-correlated subquery, inner subquery has no dependency on outer query.

50. Given an Employee table with Manager_ID as column, print First name, Manager ID and Level of employees in Organization Structure?

Answer: In Oracle, we can CONNECT BY clause for this.

The starting point will be the employee who does not have a manager. Below that we can connect the employee IDs with their Manager IDs and keep printing the records.

Oracle provides a pseudocolumn LEVEL that gives the

level of each record in hierarchy.

Query will be as follows:

SELECT f_name, emp_id, manager_id, LEVEL

    FROM Employee

    START WITH emp_id = 10

    CONNECT BY PRIOR emp_id = manager_id;

F_NAME	EMP_ID	MANAGER_ID	LEVEL
John	10		1
George	14	10	2
Jill	16	14	3
Bill	15	14	3
Jay	18	14	3

Bonus Question:

51.   Write a query to create an empty table from an existing table?

Answer: An empty table is a table with same structure as the given table. But it does not contain records.

To create an empty table, we have to run a SELECT query so that no records are returned. But we can use the result of this query in CREATE statement to create an empty table.

To get no records in SELECT query, we can give a false condition like 1 > 2 in WHERE clause.

Query will be as follows:

CREATE TABLE Test_table AS

        SELECT * from Src_table

        WHERE 1 > 2;

Thanks!!!

We hope you liked our book. Please help us by giving your valuable review on Amazon.com.

Your review will mean a lot to us!!

REFERENCES

https://docs.oracle.com/cd/B12037_01/server.101/b10759/ap_standard_sql001.htm

https://docs.oracle.com/cd/B19306_01/server.102/b14200/toc.htm

Made in the USA
San Bernardino, CA
07 April 2017